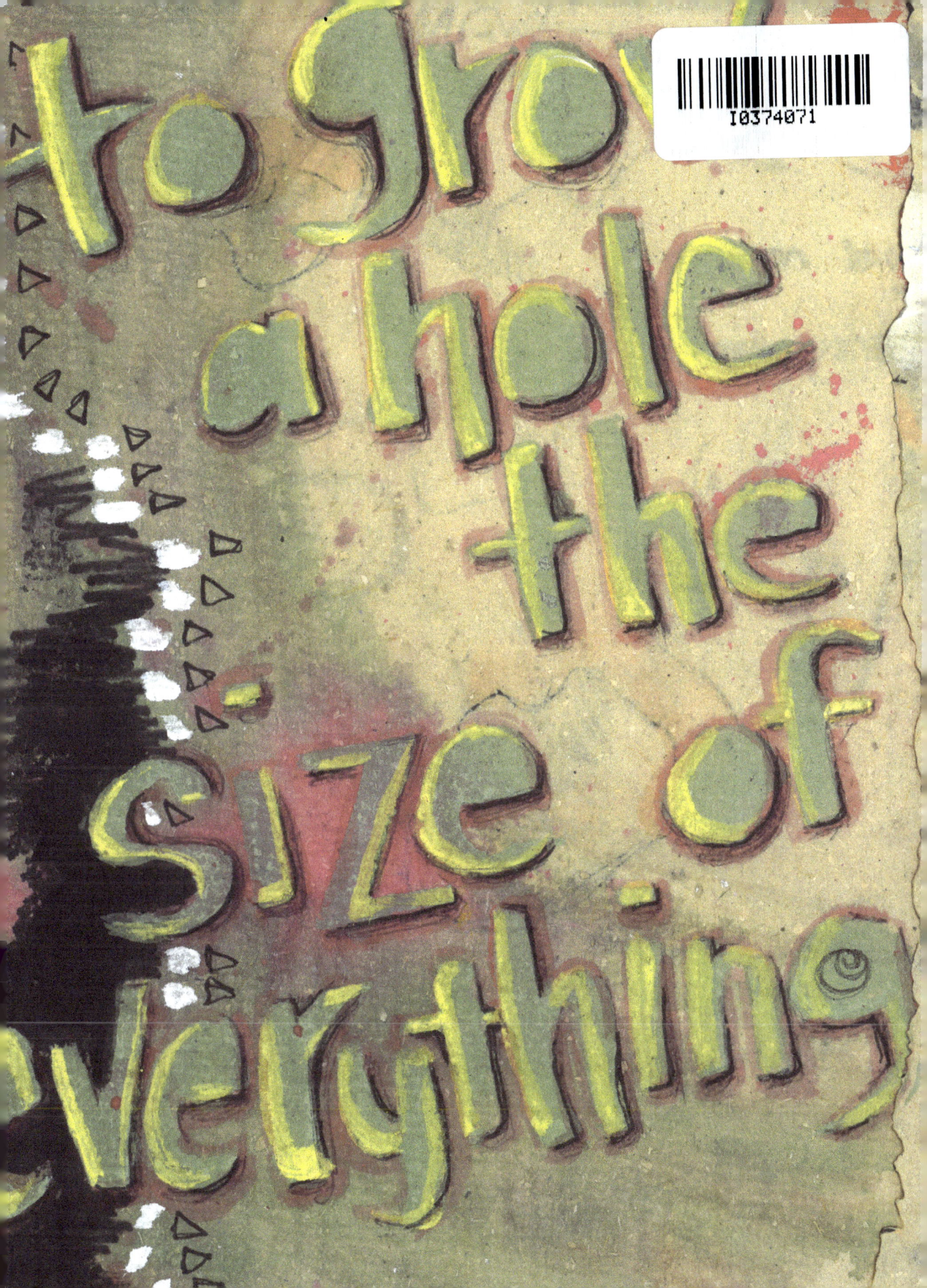

Stubborn Mule Press
Devil's Elbow, MO
stubbornmulepress.com

poem copyright © Jason Preu 2019
jason.preu@icloud.com
art copyright © Jeanette Powers 2019
strange.gen.et@gmail.com

First Edition 11 7 5 3 2 1
ISBN: 978-1-950380-38-1

Are you really reading this? Congratulations, we love you. No one but the author can really claim rights to their work, no matter what law says what. And we can't really do anything about theft, whatever that means, so here is our pact: Be cool, be kind, don't steal, email the author if you like or want to riff off their work. Also, let us at Stubborn Mule know if you want to write a review, we'll share it and your review publication, too. Go ahead and use passages for reviews, accolades, or epigraphs, give credit where credit is due. Let's stay radical, share with us our honor among anarchists.

cut outs by Man Ray

Start with a mote: ○ ◎ ・

what is a mote?

infinitely dense;

@ *hefty pixel..*

ough
he
TE

@ MOTE

contains
us
ALL

this word
this word
this word
this word

this
word
sublime

this
word
sublime

c
cra
crav
crave
cave
clavin
raven
crave
rave
crave
raven
crave
crave

mote
missed?

BUT
WHAT
COULD
IT
CRAVE

what
COULD
it crave ??? ?//? ?

AND everything—

and ... (sigh)

everything →

AND is is

to warm,

NOW THIS MOTE

contemplates death by volition.

to grow.

NOW THIS MOTE

memorizes

every line

of

every

play.

Sweet

the MOTE whimpers, thinks about no things,

MOTE

shvdders

A RIPPED RECLAMATION OF

to be!

the

FRIGHTENED BY REAL *possibilities* IN EXISTENCE.

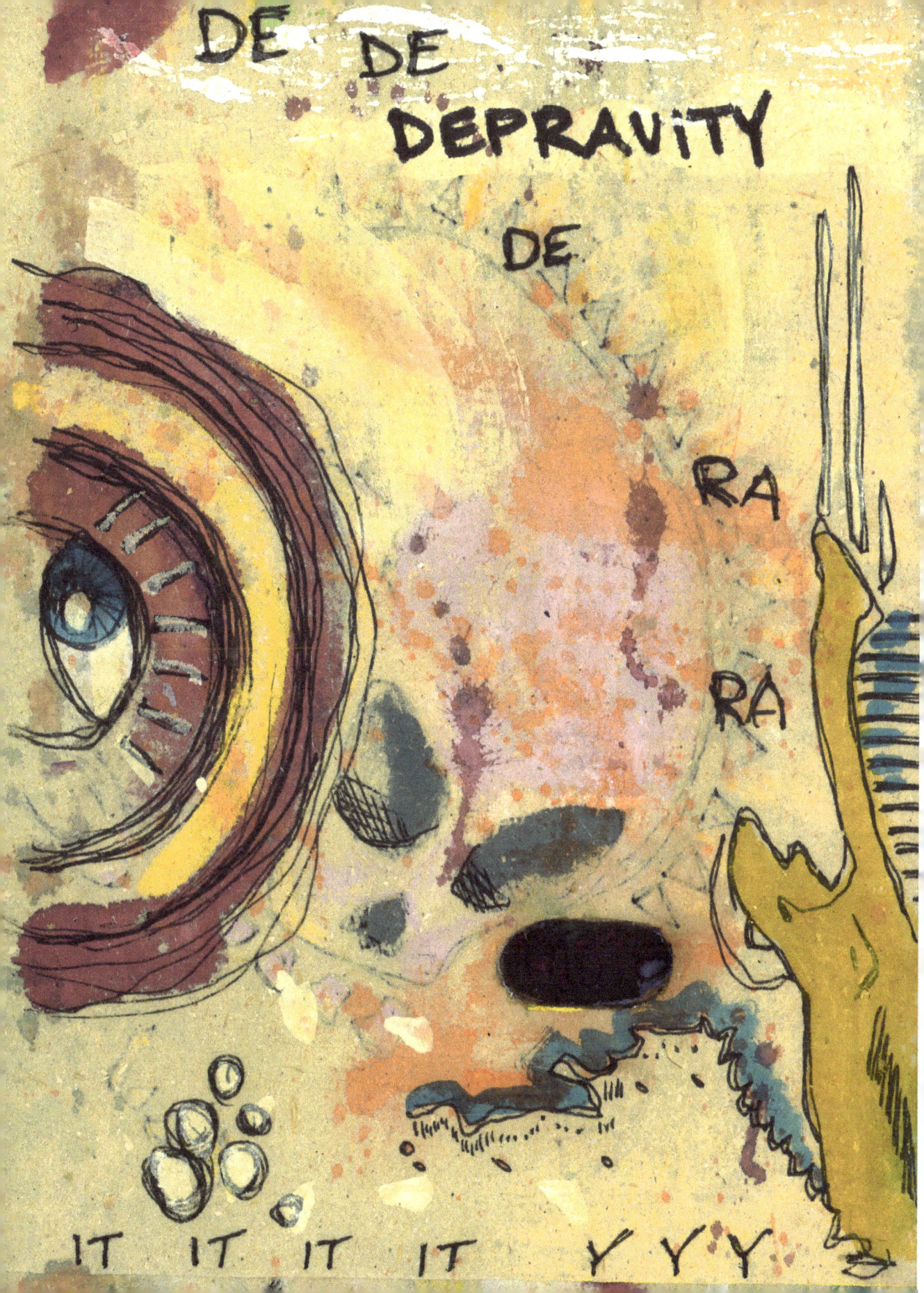

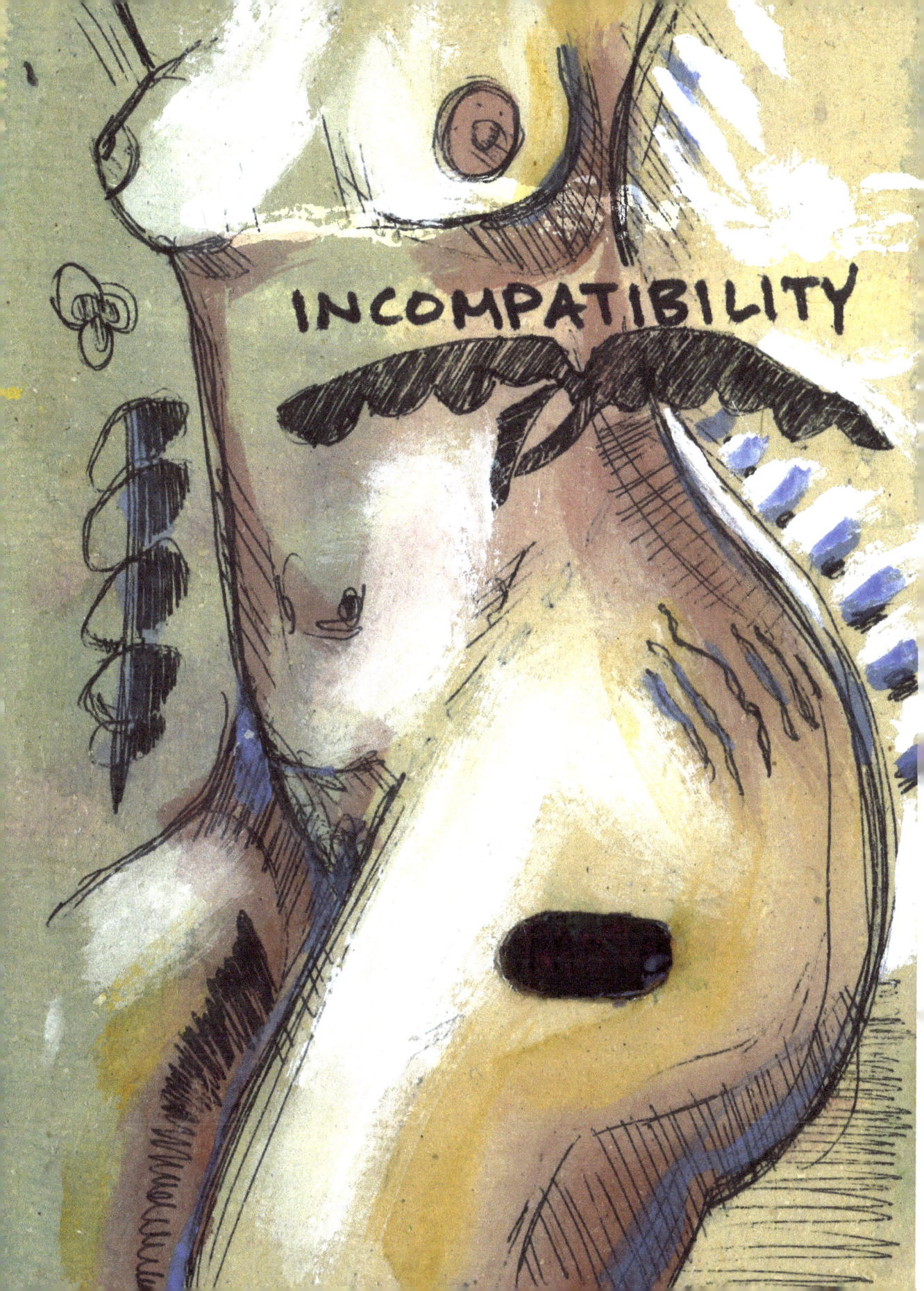

LONGEVITY.

SWIRL

EXPANSION

COLLISION

COLLUSION

COALESCING ACTUALITY.

TRIPS
HEAD OVER HEELS
INTO
AN
ENEVERATED
MARCH
ONWARD

AND

FOREVER
EVER
ONWARD

RECONSIDERS

go.
go.

reconsiders, lets go,

with the IMPOSSIBILITY OF RESPONSIBILITY FOR everything itself.

NOTE

the

MOTE
shudders

www.ingramcontent.com/pod-product-compliance
Lightning Source LLC
Chambersburg PA
CBHW051334110526
44591CB00026B/3002